You don't have to have a dream

To my Dad.

You don't have to have a dream
TIM MINCHIN

Illustrations by Andrew Rae
Designed by Dave Brown

EBURY
PRESS

6

Now look, the cynic in me knows that universities hand out honorary degrees in order to generate publicity. We all know the deal: some so-called celeb gets a gaudy gown and a floppy beret and, in return, they give an address, and hopefully it's good, and if it is (and the PR folk are on their game), the uni gets a bit of attention.

A fair trade: fancy words for fancy hats.

But cynicism is *so* early 2020s and there are shamefully few scenarios these days where you can rock a silk cape and properly get away with it, so I choose to be proud of my pseudoctorates.

(In fact, I have accepted three of them, so – although both my father and his father before him were surgeons – I am indisputably the greatest Dr Minchin ever. And because I understand that greatness comes with responsibility, I offer you this pledge: if we're on a plane together and you have a heart attack and the crew call for a doctor, I shall leap to your aid. At the very least, I can pitch you a few options for whimsical dying words.)

This book contains the three Occasional Addresses I've made for the three very kind institutions who thought me worthy of Floppyhat Funtimes™. In basic terms, there's one about being human, one about being a musician, and one about being an actor. I have some experience of being all of these things, arguably concurrently, so I suppose the hubris is justified or, at least, forgivable.

Reflecting on the three speeches now, I notice they are reasonably complementary and cohesive, if not a little over-lappy. My science-loving, pragmatic-progressive, reality-romantic worldview bullies its way into all of them, as it does into so much of my work, as it will into my introductions.

A part of me was concerned that these addresses wouldn't work in text, stripped as they are of my carefully honed rhetorical flourishlessness. But so many people over the years have told me that they've printed bits of them out, or have phrases written on sticky notes above their desks, or quote them in their classrooms and lecture halls. So I'm thrilled there's now an artefact: a tightly bound version of me you can keep by the loo.

Right where I belong.

Tim Minchin, June 2024

Nine
Life
Lessons

University of Western Australia, 2013

I was only just seventeen when I started at the University of Western Australia, and only just twenty when I skulked out of there with a lukewarm Bachelor of Arts. In the intervening three years, all my essays and analyses and creative writing pieces were executed under the self-imposed extreme pressure of the pro-procrastinator, and things haven't changed much in the ensuing decades.

I wrote the speech that came to be known as 'Nine Life Lessons' in the forty-eight hours before I was to be presented with an Honorary Degree of Doctor of Letters at UWA in 2013. By then I was thirty-eight, a full five years older than Jesus managed, so I felt more than qualified to mount the mount and sermonise a bit. I can't remember if I knew someone was taping it, but if I'd known it was going to be viewed a couple of hundred million times, I might have thought about it a bit more.

Which is probably a pretty good argument for not thinking about shit too much.

In the decade since, both the world and my view of it have altered (the former, a lot, the latter, a little), and if I were writing this speech today, I might have a slightly different focus. I would certainly feel compelled to bang on about the corrosive influence of social media on social cohesion, its tendency to corral people towards closed-minded extremes.

But I wouldn't need to change a lot, because although how we communicate our ideas has changed, the tools we need to fight the bad ones have not.

My Christmas song, 'White Wine in the Sun', has this line:

I don't go in for ancient wisdom,

I don't believe just 'cos ideas are tenacious it means
that they're worthy.

It's a nice lyric, I reckon, but not an original critique:
in philosophy, an *argument from antiquity* is the claim
that the *age* of an idea is an indicator of its *validity*.
This fallacy still rears its head, but recently I've become
more concerned about the popularity of the opposite error.
We seem to be in an era that wants to throw out old ideas
just *because* they're old, and perhaps because they have
failed to deliver utopia.

We should be wary, though. There are a lot of useful
babies in history's fetid ol' bathwater.

My worldview, though ever-evolving, is rooted in pretty
old-school values: the importance of critical thinking
and the scientific method (which together counteract our
many biases); the painful necessity of a free marketplace
of ideas (even ideas we find abhorrent); a fundamental
antipathy towards restricted speech *and* compelled speech
(however well-meaning); and other important heuristics.
These 'enlightenment' values were not a top-down political
ideology invented by European men, but an intellectual
gestalt that emerged out of the accumulated cross-cultural
wisdom of the ages.

These values don't guarantee instant fixes, and perhaps
because of understandable frustration with the slow rate of
change, they are currently being casually discarded by both
the populist-reactionary right and the post-modernism-addled
left. But I believe they remain an irreplaceable set of tools.

12

No religion, no political ideology, no war nor revolution has ever been as conducive to progress as this simple notion: that we should treat our assumptions with scepticism, and stay open to new ideas and information. It's a paradigm that has the massive advantage of baked-in fluidity and – across the long arc – incremental improvement. It facilitates memetic evolution. It is fundamentally anti-doctrinal, demanding of us epistemic, intellectual, psychological, neurological and cultural humility. (Post-modernism, to its credit, contributed much to that last one.)

Stir in a couple of ideas like the Principle of Charity (listening to the views of others with the generosity you'd like to be listened to), and a dedication to rejecting in-group/out-group thinking, and you've got yourself a sweet little recipe for societal flourishing.

Old bathwater, evergreen babies, baby.

Because I hold a passionate – probably naïve – belief in **art** as the most powerful method by which we can share valuable ideas, it is unsurprising that these values end up in my work. And not just in my speeches and stand-up comedy rants. In 2009 I wrote this satirical lyric for *Matilda the Musical*, sung by the horrendous Mrs Wormwood in 'Loud':

> *What you know matters less,*
> *Than the volume with which what you don't*
> *know's expressed*
>
> *Content has never been less important, so… you have*
> *got to be LOUD.*

The same year, in 'The Fence':

> *We divide the world to stop us feeling frightened*

> *Into wrong and into right and*
> *Into black and into white.*

Almost fifteen years later, again in full-blown satire mode for 'Play It Safe',

> *You gotta work out who your team is, and wear the badge with pride!*
>
> *Find a box that makes you comfortable and then stay the heck inside!*
>
> *Toe the line, don your suit, hide your truth, wipe your tears,*
>
> *Don't cause trouble, find your bubble, stick to black and white ideas,*
>
> *Play it safe, know your place, know your lines, know your limits,*
>
> *Find a doctrine, get it locked in, build a box and stay in it!*

And in countless examples in between, in 'Storm' and 'Fifteen Minutes of Shame' and 'Thank You God' and 'Stuck', and in my BAFTAs opening, and in many podcasts and interviews – there simmers an entreaty to think critically, to embrace a system of self-correction, to be wary of bubbles and extremes.

To seek truth, to hold it tightly, but to be prepared to relax your grip if new information comes to light.

The tides change, but the epistemic rudder I use to negotiate them remains a pretty darn good one. The *Nine Lessons* metaphors of cricket bats and tennis courts still hold, I think.

*

In darker days, I did a corporate gig
at a conference for this big company
who made and sold accounting software.
In a bid, I presume, to inspire their
salespeople to greater heights,
they'd forked out 12 grand for an
inspirational speaker who was this
extreme sports dude who had
had a couple of his limbs frozen
off when he got stuck on a ledge
on some mountain.

It was weird.

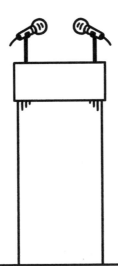

16   Surely software salespeople need to hear from someone who has had a long, successful and happy career in software sales, not from an overly optimistic ex-mountaineer.

And if the mountain was meant to be a symbol of life's challenges, and the loss of limbs a metaphor for sacrifice, the software guy's not going to get it, is he? 'Cos he didn't do an arts degree, did he? He should have. Arts degrees are awesome. They help you find meaning where there is none. And let me assure you, there is none. Don't go looking for it. Searching for meaning is like searching for a rhyme scheme in a cookbook: you won't find it and you'll bugger up your soufflé.

Point being, I'm not an inspirational
speaker. I've never lost a limb on
a mountainside, metaphorically
or otherwise. And I'm certainly not
here to give career advice, 'cos… well,
I've never really had what most would
call a Proper Job.

However, I *have* had large groups
of people listening to what I say for
quite a few years now, and it's given
me an inflated sense of self-importance.
So I will now – at the ripe old age
of thirty-eight – bestow upon you
nine life lessons. To echo, of course,
the nine lessons and carols of the
traditional Christmas service.
Which is also pretty obscure.

18 You might find some of this stuff inspiring, you will find some of it boring, and you will definitely forget all of it within a week.
And be warned, there will be lots of hokey similes, and obscure aphorisms which start well but end up making no sense.

So listen up, or you'll get lost, like a blind man clapping in a pharmacy trying to echo-locate the contact lens fluid.

Here we go...

1.
You Don't Have to Have a Dream

22 Americans on talent shows always talk about their dreams. Fine, if you have something that you've always dreamed of, like, in your heart, go for it! After all, it's something to do with your time... chasing a dream. And if it's a big enough one, it'll take you most of your life to achieve, so by the time you get to it and are staring into the abyss of the meaninglessness of your achievement you'll be almost dead, so it won't matter.

I never really had one of these
big dreams. I advocate passionate
dedication to the pursuit of short-term
goals. Be micro-ambitious. Put your
head down and work with pride on
whatever is in front of you... You never
know where you might end up. Just
be aware that the next worthy pursuit
will probably appear in your periphery.
Which is why you should be careful
of long-term dreams. If you focus too
far in front of you, you won't see the
shiny thing out the corner of your eye.

Right?

Good. Advice. Metaphor.

Look at me go.

2.
Don't
Seek
Happiness

26

Happiness is like an orgasm: if you think about it too much, it goes away.

Keep busy and aim to make someone else happy, and you might find you get some as a side effect. We didn't evolve to be constantly content. Contented *Australopithecus afarensis* got eaten before passing on their genes.

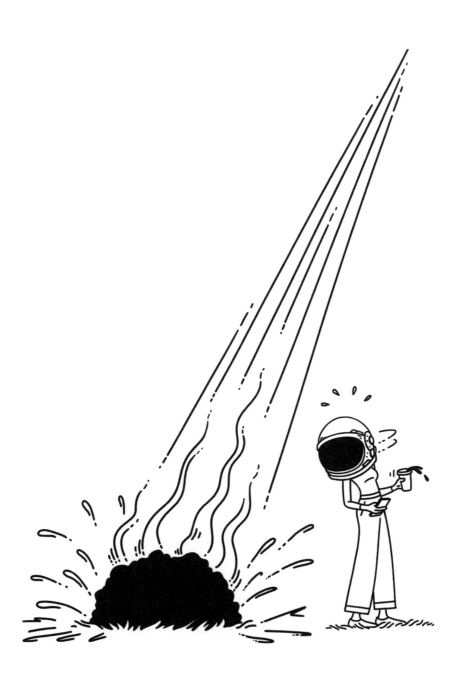

3.
Remember, It's All Luck

You are lucky to be here.

You were incalculably lucky to be born, and incredibly lucky to be brought up by a nice family that helped you get educated and encouraged you to go to university. Or if you were born into a horrible family, that's unlucky and you have my sympathy… but you were still lucky: lucky that you happened to be made of the sort of DNA that made the sort of brain which – when placed in a horrible childhood environment – would make decisions that meant you ended up, eventually, graduating from university. Well done you, for dragging yourself up by the shoelaces. But you were lucky.

You didn't create the bit of you that dragged you up. **They're not even your shoelaces.** I suppose I worked hard to achieve whatever dubious achievements I've achieved… but I didn't make the bit of me that works hard, any more than I made the bit of me that ate too many burgers instead of going to lectures.

Understanding that you can't truly take credit for your successes, nor truly blame others for their failures, will humble you and make you more compassionate. Empathy is intuitive, but is also something that you can work on, intellectually.

4.
Exercise!

34

I'm sorry, you pasty, pale, smoking philosophy grads, arching your eyebrows into a Cartesian curve as you watch the Human Movement mob winding their way through the miniature traffic cones of their existence: you are wrong and they are right. Well, you're half right – you think, therefore you are... but also: you jog, therefore you sleep well, therefore you're not overwhelmed by existential angst. You can't be Kant, and you don't want to be.

Play a sport, do yoga, pump iron, run...
whatever... but take care of your body.
You're going to need it. Most of you mob
are going to live to nearly a hundred, and
even the poorest of you will achieve a level
of wealth that most humans throughout
history could not have dreamed of. And this
long, luxurious life ahead of you is going to
make you depressed!

But don't despair! There is an inverse
correlation between depression and exercise.

Do it.
Run, my beautiful intellectuals, run.

And don't smoke.
Natch.

5.
Be
Hard
On Your
Opinions

38   A famous bon mot asserts that opinions are like arseholes, in that everyone has one. There is great wisdom in this... but I would add that opinions differ significantly from arseholes, in that yours should be constantly and thoroughly examined.

We must think critically, and not just about the ideas of others. Be hard on your beliefs. Take them out onto the veranda and hit them with a cricket bat. Be intellectually rigorous. Identify your biases, your prejudices, your privileges.

Most of society's arguments are kept alive by a failure to acknowledge nuance. We tend to generate false dichotomies, then try to argue one point using two entirely different sets of assumptions, like two tennis players trying to win a match by hitting beautifully executed shots from either end of separate tennis courts.

By the way, while I have science and arts grads
in front of me: please don't make the mistake
of thinking the arts and sciences are at odds
with one another. That is a recent, stupid and
damaging idea. You don't have to be unscientific
to make beautiful art or to write beautiful things.

If you need proof: Twain, Adams, Vonnegut,
McEwan, Sagan, Shakespeare, Dickens. For a
start. You don't need to be superstitious to be
a poet. You don't need to hate GM technology
to care about the beauty of the planet. You don't
have to claim a soul to promote compassion.

Science is not a body of knowledge nor
a system of belief; it is just a term which
describes humankind's incremental acquisition
of understanding through observation.

Science is awesome.

40 The arts and sciences need to
work together to improve how
knowledge is communicated.
The idea that many still believe
that the science of anthropogenic
global warming is controversial
is a powerful indicator of the extent
of our failure to communicate.
(The fact that 30 per cent of this
room just bristled is further evidence
still. The fact that that bristling
is more to do with politics than
science is even more despairing.)

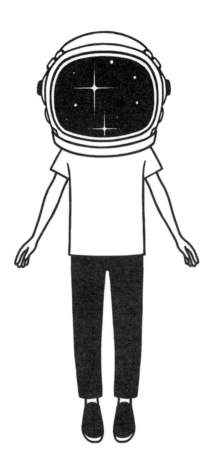

6.
Be a
Teacher

44 **P**lease? Please be a teacher. Teachers are the most admirable and important people in the world. You don't have to do it forever, but if you're in doubt about what to do, be an amazing teacher. Just for your twenties. Be a primary-school teacher.

Especially if you're a
bloke – we need male
primary-school teachers.
Even if you're not a
teacher, be a teacher.
Share your ideas.
Don't take for granted
your education.
Rejoice in what you learn,
and spread it.

7.
Define Yourself By What You Love

48 I've found myself doing this thing a bit recently, where, if someone asks me what sort of music I like, I say, 'Well, I don't listen to the radio because pop lyrics annoy me.' Or if someone asks me what food I like, I say, 'I think truffle oil is overused and slightly obnoxious.' I see it all the time online, people whose idea of being part of a subculture is to hate Coldplay or football or feminists or the Liberal Party. We have a tendency to define ourselves in opposition to stuff; as a comedian, I make a living out of it. But try to also express your passion for things you love. Be demonstrative and generous in your praise of those you admire. Send thank-you cards and give standing ovations.

Be pro-stuff,

not
just
anti-stuff.

8.
Respect People With Less Power Than You

52 I have, in the past,
made important decisions
about people I work with –
agents and producers –
based largely on how they
treat wait staff in restaurants.
I don't care if you're the most
powerful cat in the room,
I will judge you on how you
treat the least powerful.
So there.

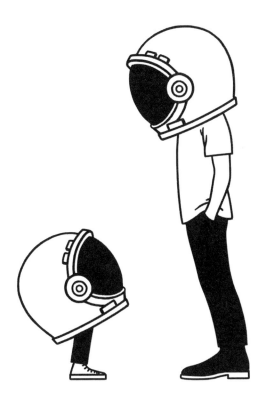

9.
Don't
Rush

56 You don't need to already know what you're going to do with the rest of your life. I'm not saying sit around smoking cones all day, but also, don't panic. Most people I know who were sure of their career path at twenty are having midlife crises now.

58 I said at the beginning of this ramble that life is meaningless. It was not a flippant assertion. I think it's absurd, the idea of seeking 'meaning' in the set of circumstances that happens to exist after 13.8 billion years' worth of unguided events. Leave it to humans to think the universe has a purpose for them. However, I am no nihilist. I am not even a cynic. I am, actually, rather romantic. And here's my idea of romance:

You will soon be dead.

60   Life will sometimes seem long and tough and, God, it's tiring. And you will sometimes be happy and sometimes sad. And then you'll be old. And then you'll be dead.

There is only one sensible thing to do with this empty existence, and that is: fill it.

(Not fillet. Fill. It.)

And in my opinion (until I change it), life is best filled by learning as much as you can about as much as you can, taking pride in whatever you're doing, having compassion, sharing ideas, running(!), being enthusiastic.

WHO'S THE WORLD
GOING TO REVOLVE
AROUND NOW?

And then there's

love,

and travel,

and wine,

and sex,

and art,

and kids,

and giving,

and mountain climbing...

but you know all that stuff already.

62 It's an incredibly exciting thing, this one, meaningless life of yours.

Good luck.

The
Trick

The Western Australian Academy of Performing Arts, 2019

INTRODUCTION

By the time I'd turned twenty-one, I had written five
or six scores for youth and university theatre, a couple
of soundtracks for short films and documentaries, and
countless songs for my various bands... and I decided
it was high time I learned to read music!

So in 1996, in between writing tunes and acting in amateur
plays and working in bars and cafés, I got an audition for
a new Commercial Music course at the Western Australian
Academy of Performing Arts and, despite misremembering
the audition time and turning up late and furious with
myself, I played a sweaty-fingered jazz 12-bar and
a showy original instrumental that is now lost to time,
and somehow they let me in.

As it transpires, I graduated still unable to read music
(I was way too far gone), but I learned a lot about
harmony, both musical and existential. It took a good
few years for me to figure out how to apply either to
good effect.

In 2019, WAAPA invited me to a ceremony in a
Spiegeltent, a beautiful wood-and-canvas, mirrored cabaret
tent that lived for a time on campus. Having played many
gigs in Spiegels in the early days of my comedy career,
the venue filled me with nostalgia, and with horror, too:
spiegel is German for 'mirror', and being observed by
several of your own heads whilst making a speech is
pretty discombobulating.

The ceremony started with a hugely moving Nyoongar
Welcome to Country and some gorgeous student
performances, and I'd already cried twice before I got up.

Home sometimes hurts.

The dominant themes in 'The Trick' are resilience, authenticity and kindness, and in hindsight, perhaps I didn't quite articulate the relationship between the three.

I wonder if I hadn't quite joined the dots myself. My 14-yr-old is away on camp at the moment, a nine-day adventure in the mountains with sheets of plastic for tents and the weather forecast promising plenty of rain. Before he left, I reminded him that it's easy to be selfless and gregarious when things are going well, but that kindness is most valuable when the shit hits the fan (or the rain floods the sleeping bag, as it were). To square the triangle (and at the risk of sounding untrendily Kiplingy): if you can maintain kindness when your resilience is being tested, then you will be authentic, my son.

Being an artist is a Joy-and-a-Privilege™, but the personal nature of the work leaves you vulnerable to beatings. Eighteen months before I wrote the WAAPA speech, I had lost four years of some of my best work when the new studio owners binned an animated musical film I was helping to write and direct in LA (and for which my family had moved across the world... again). In the upper echelons of commercial art, where budgets are in the tens of millions, things get ruthless. This is predictable and explicable, but I really believe you can make big commercial art and still maintain plenty of ruth.

After leaving Hollywood in 2017, we moved back to Australia and I threw myself into co-writing a TV show

68   called *Upright*. It was during the editing of season 1 that I
was invited to speak at WAAPA and, as you will see, I talk
about authenticity like this:

> *We carry our scars and our defeats and victories into
> how we express ourselves. We bring all our experience,
> all our hours, all our self-loathing and self-love into our
> craft. At least we should.*

And here it gets meta, because this idea – that our
scratches and imperfections are fundamental to who we
are – is written into *Upright*. I was feeling battered and
worn after my Hollywood experience, and so, rather than
go to therapy, I chucked it all into the work. In the final
episode, when my character, Lucky, is gifting an old
upright piano to young Billie, he says:

> *I know it doesn't look fantastic, but it sounds good,
> still, believe it or not. It's got its own special sound.
> And all those dings and scratches and stuff, they're all
> part of why it sounds the way it does, you know? ...
> And (when you play) you can make heaps of mistakes.
> Don't ever worry about that, because when you muck
> up, that's when you sometimes find you've made
> something accidentally beautiful. Sometimes.*

And – meta upon meta – the song that Lucky sings in the
desert (which we eventually realise he wrote for Billie) is
called 'Carry You', and returns to the theme:

And reflected in your eyes is all my love and all my lies
Is all my promise and my pride, is all my fear and
all my fight
Is all my dread and my denial.
So though we cannot be together, I know
That I will carry you wherever I go.

We carry our shit. And if we're smart, and lucky enough to be artists, we can use our shit as fertiliser. Maybe grow something beautiful.

THE TRICK

So this week I'm staying at the Casino, which is not my usual vibe, but the theatre I'm playing is in the building, and besides, if I stay with my parents, the kettle wakes me up at half-past six and I'm not having that. Anyway, presumably because my tour is attracting punters, the hotel management upgraded me, so I'm staying in some kind of penthouse suite thing that's about the size of my house and I feel like I'm living in an Italian furniture showroom. There are just so many couches. I'm staying there on my own, yet I counted and you could have ninety people comfortably sitting in my hotel room. I don't know what it's for. It's a room built for the sole purpose of making Wankers feel like Legends. Trump would love it.

When you first walk into a room like that you initially feel really excited, but it's genuinely gross and quite miserable to stay there. That's worth knowing, I guess, if your plan is to be a rock star or a famous actor. It's not only lonely at the top, but populated by unnecessary chairs. Put that on a fridge magnet.

My time here at WAAPA was quite hard, actually. Being an artist requires massive reserves of self-belief, and coming to a place like this is incredibly testing. Of course, I know now that the two years I spent here feeling unbelievably bad about myself were simply training for the subsequent eight years where I felt even worse. Watching Graham Wood play piano and just wanting to give up – wanting to cut my fingers off and feed them to a swan – taught me... well, not to, I guess.

It was the beginning of a lesson I'm still trying
to learn:

comparing yourself to others in any area of your life is poison.

It was also hard here because I had really good friends in the acting course, and they were all wandering around in black tights and shagging each other and looking fabulously sweaty while I was wandering around with the other pianist in my year, who was a sweet guy, but profoundly pessimistic, and every day just reminded me how we were going to be poor for life. And it was hard because, like you, I was making coffees and pouring beers to pay my rent, but mostly it was hard because, until then, music had always just been fun to me.

74 Music was a thing you did at parties
to pick up girls. It was something
I did when I was stressed or sad.
It was an escape. I could (and still
can) fall asleep playing the piano and
wake up seconds later wondering
how my fingers got to where they'd
got. But coming here it was work,
suddenly. I had to *practise*. (The first
year I was here remains the only year
I ever actually practised piano. Russell
Holmes will confirm I certainly
didn't do any practice in second year.
Somewhere in the first few weeks it
became clear we both preferred just
hanging out and chatting!)

But I am so grateful for the two years
I spent here. It's almost impossible to
measure the value of what that diploma
gave me.

Much of what they were teaching me I couldn't get at the time, but unconsciously I put the info on some shelf in my brain to be picked up and properly examined later when I had more time and was feeling less stubborn. I learnt musical tools, performance tools. I learnt to respect time, I learnt to listen, I learnt resilience. I learnt that dominant thirteenth shape that is also a minor six-nine, and a dominant seven sharp five sharp nine and a major seven sharp eleven, and that's the best shape in the world and *Matilda* is built on it.

I never learnt to read music. I don't know whose failure that is. I guess I'm trying to say to the students here: I know these places can be hard, but keep going. You won't actually know what you're really learning until years later.

Just listen, keep your humility and stay tough.

78   Right. If this were a graduation ceremony,
       my role here would be to give career advice to the
       graduates. It's not, but I guess I'll try to give advice
       anyway because I'm quite old now and giving
       unsolicited advice is what old white guys are
       supposed to do. I'm going to mansplain the Arts
       to you. It's actually surprising to me how often
       I get asked for career advice. Young musos and
       actors and parents of stagey little kids, they go:

'How do you get a career like you?'

And I mean, I get it. I so clearly remember in my
teens and twenties thinking:

'What's the trick?
There must be a trick.'

But it still takes me aback when they ask me,
because my career is so clearly such an
absurd fluke.

I mean, I simply got lucky. And not lucky like I was on a bus and got my umbrella confused with the umbrella of a guy who turned out to be the husband of a record company exec. There was no single moment of luck, nor a series of lucky events. I mean, it's a fluke, because it turned out that having my weird combination of attributes allowed me to make some stuff that happened to find an audience in a particular place and time. And that's the short and long of my advice, really.

There is no trick.
You can't have a career like mine.
It's mine.
You have to have *your* career.

To expand on that platitude, I'll tell you three things I reckon are important if you're serious about a career in musical theatre or dance or film. All three of these are total clichés, but perhaps worth reiterating.

80 Firstly, you have to **get good.**
Get *really* good. No shortcut, no business
technique, no amount of self-promotion
or nice business cards. None of it
means anything, really. You just have
to be really, really good at what you
do. Ideally, be the best. And that takes
hours and hours and hours, time when
your mates are taking pills or smoking
cones, time when other people are having
holidays. You don't get to have a good
work-life balance. It means being
a bit obsessed, and if you're lucky
it won't suck because you love it.

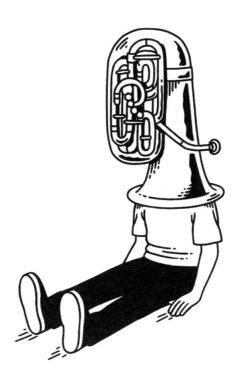

And if you don't love it, stop now.

82   Don't do it as a job. There are many more important jobs
than being a muso, or an actor, or at least *as* important.
Get one of those and play music as a hobby. But if you're
going to make a career of it, you simply have to spend all
your time and all your energy and all your money getting
good. Sorry.

There is, however, a little loophole in this advice,
which is that how you define 'what you do' is up to you.
I am the best in the world at what I do without a doubt,
and I can say that confidently because the number of people
I am competing with is zero.

The thing I am best in the world at is being a science-obsessed uber-rhymey polemicist pianist singer-satirist wanker.

I am really, really good at that job. I am the king of
Minchinland, population: this idiot. So be really, really
good at what you do, and figuring out what that is also
takes hours and hours and hours. I'm sorry.

And this is related to my second bit of advice, which is that
you have to **be authentic.** Actors, you might
authentically look like a Hemsworth and authentically love
going to the gym, but I promise, as someone who's been
involved in casting on both sides of the couch,
all anyone wants to see is you. We want to see how you
play the character, how you bring you into a character.
My career began in my late twenties when I finally stopped
trying to be what I thought other people wanted from me.
I was trying to get acting agents, getting headshots and
cutting my hair, changing my name to Timothy as if any
of that crap ever changed anything.

84   I was trying to get the silliness out of my songs
in the hope that I could get a record deal. I was
separating all the things I am, because I had
identified what I thought was the marketplace
available to me, and I was trying to be various
products that might be consumable. The minute –
the *minute* – I stuck everything I am on the stage,
the moment I wore what I wanted, said what
I wanted, put together a show that had me doing
weird poems and monologues and playing jazz
and pop and rock, **the moment I got**
authentic, my life changed.
I'm an odd example, obviously, because I've always
been obsessed by trying to do lots of different
things, but the lesson stands anyway. In your career
– whether you want to be a triple threat on the
West End or a film actor or a session percussionist
– don't make the mistake of thinking that little old
you is not interesting to the world.

You have lived a unique life, consumed a unique suite of ideas, marinated in a unique combination of songs and artists and influences. You will have something that no one else has, and identifying that is your key to a beautiful career. That career might mean you are dirt-poor your whole life, or it might mean you get to be a massive star, but it won't matter because you won't be trying to be something that you're not.

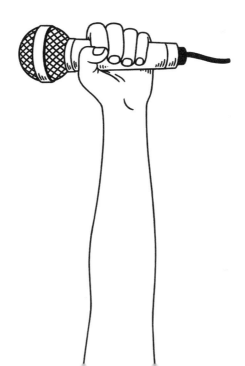

86 And the third bit of advice: **be kind.**
Just be kind to everyone, always.
Actually, you don't have to be kind
upwards. You'll come across people
above you – a director or a producer
or a studio boss, an A&R dude –
who are arseholes, and you're allowed
to tell them to fuck off. But basically
you should always be kind. It seems
so obvious, but it's amazing how many
people fail to understand its importance.
Be kind to the monitor guys, be kind
to the fly mech, be kind to the ushers
and the merch people, the gaffers,
the makeup artists. Be kind to your
fellow performers whatever happens.

Even if there is feedback screaming in your in-ears, even if the air con doesn't work in your trailer and you're freezing, even if you're under huge pressure and you've under-slept and you're working days and gigging nights and you haven't written a speech you have to write, and you're starving and all you want is some poached eggs and a flat white delivered to your furniture-store hotel room but you've accidentally left your do-not-disturb sign on the door so the waiter just doesn't deliver your breakfast for an hour and then when he does he spills your flat white onto your poached eggs – even then, be kind.

If in doubt, double down and be kinder. Not only will it make your life better, but it's really good career advice.

88 The musicians I'm working with on this tour are some of the best players in the country, but that's only half the reason we sought them out. They are just really, really lovely people.

So
just
be
kind.

It will bite you on the arse if you're not.

(And yes, there are successful arseholes
– I've worked with a couple of the
most famous of them – but who wants
to be one of them? It's gross.)

Look... music is not magic to me.

Being a musician is not particularly romantic. Songwriting is a craft you get better at by doing it over and over again, just like cooking or surgery or painting or sex or handstands. Our ability to make art that resonates correlates very closely to our experience in life. I'm back at authenticity now.

We carry our scars and our defeats and victories into how we express ourselves. We bring all our experience, all our hours, all our self-loathing and self-love into our craft.

At least we should.

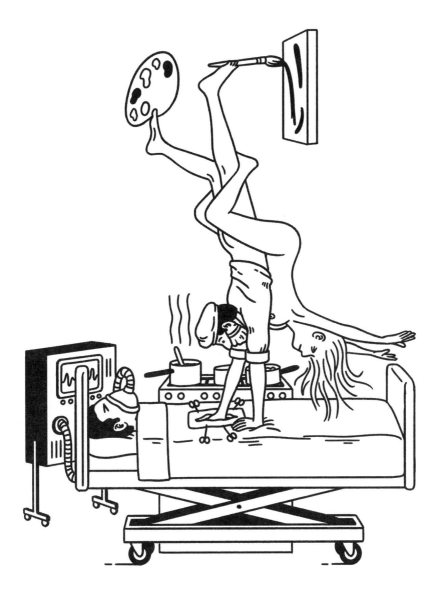

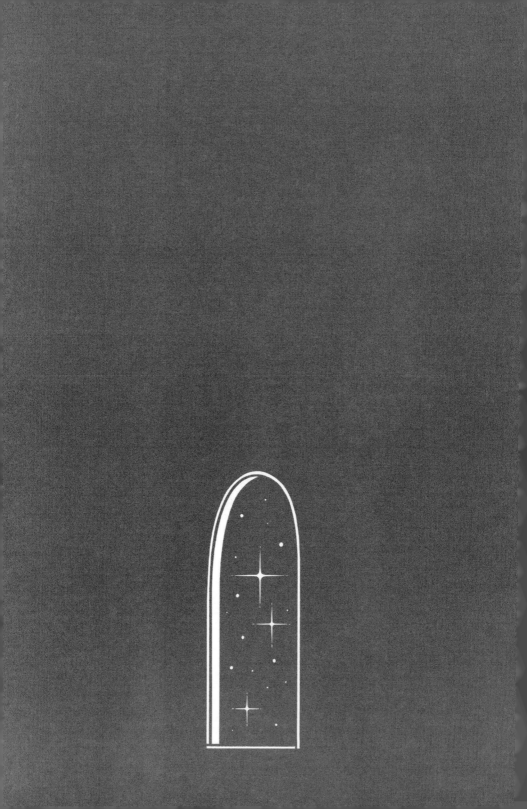

You've Always Wanted to be an Actor

Mountview Academy of Theatre Arts, London, 2015

*M*atilda the Musical opened at the Cambridge Theatre in London's West End in 2011 and has been playing there ever since. In 2015, the Mountview Academy awarded honorary doctorates to its writers, and – quid pro quo – Dennis Kelly and I were asked to speak at a graduation ceremony. The ceremony was held at the Cambridge Theatre on the amazing Rob Howell-designed *Matilda* stage (thus the phrase 'two clowns standing on the set of our mutual fluke').

I was still living and working in LA when I wrote this speech, and in it you can feel my growing discomfort with the idea of fame. Unlike many, I had actually moved to Hollywood to *escape* recognition, rather than find more of it. Sarah and I had young kids and had decided that my being spotted on the street wasn't good for them, nor useful for my own psyche. So I stepped away from the arena tours and the TV appearances, left our beloved London, and went to help write and direct a cartoon.

The eventual failure of that project, combined with my natural antipathy towards glamourised narratives, explains a lot about how snarky I was feeling in this period of my life. ('Leaving LA', written weeks before I left it, described the Hollywood sign as *just some fucking letters on a hill*, and sardonically celebrates *both its glorious dimensions*. Bitter much, Minchin?!)

In hindsight, it was probably a bit mean to paint such a dystopian picture of actorly success for the dream-filled Mountview grads of 2015 and I hope it didn't dampen anyone's drive. I suppose I was attempting to put a bit of stuffing in the mattress onto which so many of them would inevitably have to fall. I've learned since then that it's best not to do that too much. There are worse things than young eyes full of stars.

That said, I remain a dyed-in-the-wool anti-romantic romantic. I believe the world is more beautiful when seen in all its glory and gloriouslessness. Or perhaps it's more this: I think truth matters a great deal, and believe that within a truthful assessment of the human experience there is plenty of profundity, beauty and meaning to be found. Mined. Created.

Like a good student of post-modernism, I think culture is ALL narrative: we are built of the stories we choose to tell about ourselves. And yet, like a good student of science, I don't think we need these narratives to rob from reality. I don't think stories that require people to fool themselves serve us so well in the long run. At the root of my atheism – and my writing style – is a natural tendency to try to beautify ugly truths rather than swallow beautiful lies.

'Apart Together' is a song about the beauty of watching the person you love most in the world decay. *Upright*, as discussed, talks about embracing damage. In the beat poem, 'Storm', the protagonist wraps it up like this:

Isn't this enough? Just this world?
Just this... beautiful, complex, wonderfully unfathomable
natural *world?*

96

How does it so fail to hold our attention
That we have to diminish it with the invention
Of cheap, man-made myths and monsters?

Echoed by Phil Connors in *Groundhog Day*, whose lifelong search for wisdom leaves him with nothing more or less transcendent than:

I'm here.
And I'm fine.

'You've Always Wanted To Be An Actor', whilst definitely at times acerbic, celebrates people who build beautiful stories outside the dominant narrative of celebrity and glamour and red ropes and pavement handprints. The speech ends with what, for me, is totemic – the idea that I keep coming back to when I don't know what to say, or make, or promote. The thing I had to remind myself of when I sat down to write these introductions:

As artists, our job is to *put into the world valuable ideas*

Which sounds simple enough, right?

But we now have the tools to put our ideas into the world almost instantaneously. We can have an emotional reaction one moment, and the next have it published online. Are each of these expressions of feeling a little piece of art? A micro-pamphlet? A tiny free-verse poem? Should we see them as such?

Is there a fundamental difference between a 'tweet' and 'art'? Just for fun, and because I'm a crusty old clown, perhaps I can proffer this humble definition of **art** in the social-media age:

Art is any expression of an idea into which you've put a bit
of fucking effort.

It is often the fast-thinking, bias-riddled, adrenalised,
dehumanising part of our brain that tweets. It is the slow-
thinking, contemplative, creative, self-aware, humanising
part of our brain that makes art.

So if I were to use the publication of this book as an
opportunity to add a bonus Life Lesson, it might
be this:

> *A valuable idea is usually one that has been carefully*
> *considered. Our feelings are not virtuous purely by*
> *virtue of how keenly we feel them. Take time to hone*
> *your opinions, then take pride in how you express them.*

That's why we create stories and songs and plays and films
and paintings. That's why we hone a craft and learn how
to confront and cajole and seduce. That's why we work so
hard to make them laugh and think and cry.

That's what the art is for.

YOU'VE ALWAYS WANTED TO BE AN ACTOR

[Author's note: This poem is too long, but like most of what I do,
it makes up in internal rhyme what it lacks in brevity.]

You've always wanted to be an actor
And your friends and you say to each other,

*I want to act because
I think story-telling
is vital to culture,*

Or

*I want to act so
I may hold up to
society a mirror,*

And there's truth in that,
But let's be honest, you really want to act
Because it's really fun, and you quite
like being clapped

100 And inhabiting your something something

And you get your head screwed up by Stanislavski

And then recalibrated by Mamet

Or the other way round,

And you learn to scuttle across the stage

like a lizard

And to caw like a crow,

And to let yourself go

And to sing and tap and cry on cue,

And you make all your mistakes

And have sex with your classmates (and then you stop doing that),

And you *learn to find the rhythm of the bard,*

So *every iamb shines but doesn't creak,*

And you *work really hard and change the way you speak*

And you become slowly aware of these relentless waves

Of self-confidence and self-loathing

That come and come and come,

(And you think the waves will smooth out when you have success,
But they don't. So the only solution is to worry about them less.
Just by the way.)

102 So you graduate drama school and that's

amazing, brilliant, amazing,

And – as you should be – you are proud,

And at the graduation ceremony you watch two clowns

Standing on the set of their Mutual Fluke

Reading speeches that they wrote the day before

And you think, **if these idiots can succeed, anything is possible!**

Which is true, in a way,

But not in a way that should necessarily give you confidence,

Due to the randomness… of… well, Dennis.

Look at him.

God *does* clearly play dice with the universe.

And so, off you go and you get an AGENT. Yippee!

And – ooh – let's say, just hypothetically,

You're really good-looking.

You're Beautiful.

And you have been blessed, let's say, with hot genes:

You stay slim easily,

You go to the gym easily,

And you have well-spaced eyes and high cheekbones

And one of those lovely big mouths that
	kids seem to have these days.

And you have found that if you stand still in front of a camera

And look just past the shoulder of the DOP,

And think about a... cup of tea... or a tricycle...

And the light hits your well-spaced eyes and your
	high cheekbones just perfectly,

Then we, the audience, will read into your stillness

Grief, or pride, or piety. (Wow!)

104   And you're also an amazing actor…

A truthful, intelligent actor,

Hard working and skilled etc.

But that's not so much the point,

Because…

Beauty.

And so…

106   You get a role in an indie film.

I mean, first you do an advert for cheese,

And a co-op at the King's Head

(Which – although you don't know it at the time –

Will be the last theatre board you ever tread),

And then a guesty on *Coronation Street* (yay!)

And then an arc on *Holby City* (hooray!)

And... THEN a supporting role in an independent film

That ends up at Cannes and is seen

By a Rudin or a Weinstein,

And gets distributed across the USA

And so you sign with an agent at CAA,

And a manager at, I dunno, somewhere,

And they tell you that you should move to LA

because

'You will have more opportunities here'

But it's clearly because

They won't get paid
If you're doing a play
At the fucking National.
Will they?

(Just by the way.)

108

So you do. You move to LA

And you're sharing a bungalow in Silverlake

With a Canadian actress who thinks

Everything Happens For A Reason,

Which you also believe,

Because no one has ever pointed out to you

That that is a stupid thing to think.

(Just by the way.)

And as is the tradition,

You struggle for a year, coffee shop job between auditions

And then, yes!

You get a well-paid job playing a sexual assault victim on

Two episodes of season twenty-five of

Law and Order: SVU

And you buy an SUV

And you move into a mid-century-modern rental

in West Ho,

With a friend of a friend who has a band

(Four banjos, a cellist, and a DJ)

Who once played at Coachella and a YouTube vid

of one of their audience members

Choking on a corn dog went viral so now they're

Quite Popular.

110 And then (yay!),

During your second pilot season in LA,

When you're missing

The drizzly comfort of the UK spring

And your mum's on the phone telling you to
come home, darling, just come home,

You audition for a new NBC 'dramedy' –

For a character who

Doesn't say too much in the pilot, but

Great script, and sixteen great writers,
and they'll

Definitely write more for your
character after the pilot. So –

After six call-backs and weeks of anxiety,

And after being filmed with the star to test
your chemistry,

You get offered the part! And you!

Little you –

Bullied in high school for having spotty skin,

Told by your primary teachers that you need to

pull your head in

And

stop showing off,

Little you who lived with four people in a

Flat in Wood Green

And worked and worked on your craft

And you didn't give in –

You have a role in a fucking US network Television Pilot,

And you do not hesitate to sign it:

The contract that says if it goes to series

You will be committed thirty-nine weeks a year for up
    to eight years.

And yay! They make the pilot

And it gets picked up

And it goes to series and so…

Your week starts with a 4:30am pickup on a Monday,

And the crew is great and the cast is great

And although half of your day is spent in your trailer,

And it's much more boring than you'd foreseen,

You're in pretty much every scene,

Generally doing something with a

Computer-slash-Bunsen-burner-slash-non-specific-screen,

In the background,

So you're always on set, and inevitably, by week's end,

Production has fallen behind six hours,

So you don't actually get off set

For your weekend until 2am on a Saturday morning,

And you sleep all Saturday, and on Sunday you learn your sides,

And reset,

rolling,

speed…

and

action.

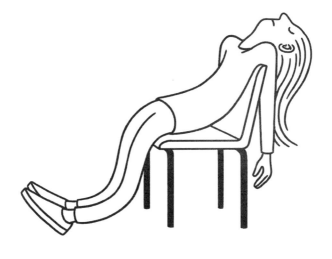

114

And that's fine.
'Cos the series is a hit!
And you're on the telly,

And the newspapers in the UK

Write about you saying something you

Don't remember saying,

And the *Daily Mail* comments on

Your hair and your abs and your arse…

And when it goes to season two, and the ratings go higher,

You get a pay rise and now you're making

A million quid a year

And you are Proper Famous,

And you are friends with Proper Famous People,

And you know Sandra and George and Bono and Elon Musk,

And you buy a fenced-in house in the hills with a pool,

And you're single, but, y'know, that's cool.

You find it hard to meet people, because, y'know

They come to you with so many assumptions about

Who you are,

About your hair and your abs and your arse.

116 And then after season three,

When the show's not quite so hot,

And the ratings start to drop,

The network gets the writers to

Simplify the script,

Cut expenses, cut the complex bits

And on they forge, churning out the eps,

Motivated by nothing but
     you-know-what,

And every year, the ratings go down a bit more,

The show loses quality a bit more,

The ideas get a bit more

Repetitive,

And your character is saying the same shit,

And you can't remember the last time

You cared about a line,

The last time you expressed an idea that had

Any. Value. Whatsoever.

118

And one Sunday, you have some of your famous friends
    around for a drink,

These beautiful, kind, generous Americans

(You do adore them but whom you always feel

You can't quite reach,

Personalities like a left-over pudding that has cling-wrap

Pulled so tight across the bowl

That you don't notice it's there at all, until you go to dig in,

And your spoon bounces off).

And so you're sitting by your pool with these

Kind, cling-film friends,

And the thought enters your head

That you'd really like to walk down the street
    to have a drink at a pub,

But you can't, because you're too famous

To leave your house.

You can't leave your house.

120

This is not a warning, to be clear;

If that becomes your story, you'll be sweet.

I wrote this because in ten years

When those of you who don't end up being

Knightley, or Laurie, or Cumberbatch…

When you have done a hundred jobs,

And, like The Boxer, you

Carry the reminder of every glove that blah blah blah

And you've borne the slings and arrows of outrageous tweets,

I hope you remember that in our game,

Success doesn't mean what They think it means.

And even if you get the type of success

That They think is success,

It won't necessarily be for the best.

122

The people I knew at your age,

The folks with whom I built sets and rigged lights

And acted and drank and dreamed,

They are... everything.

Mike is one of the finest drama teachers you would ever meet,

Jenny gathers the memories of the elderly and turns them
    into plays,

And Brian makes puppets,

And Christine runs a theatre company that tells stories of refugees,

And Tommy is a vet.

And Iggy makes music with Elders,

And Trossy is a mum,

And Justo has a million children, and paints and is a barrister

(Oh, you should hear his voice, it'd be like being defended by Lear,)

And Toby's a pirate,

And Bec runs an events company...

And to state the obvious: 123

I observe among my friends

No correlation

Between wealth and happiness

Or fame and happiness.

The happy ones work hard, generally.

And they are generous, generally.

And they generate, generally,

Valuable ideas.

Which is your job (just by the way):

To put into the world valuable ideas.

So look for stories that are worth telling

And lessons that need teaching,

And tell them and teach them,

And stay passionate,

And I'll see you at the pub.

Lots of love.

Ebury Press, an imprint of Ebury Publishing

20 Vauxhall Bridge Road London SW1V 2SA

Ebury Press is part of the Penguin Random House group of companies whose
addresses can be found at global.penguinrandomhouse.com

Penguin
Random House
UK

First published by Ebury Press in 2024

www.penguin.co.uk

A CIP catalogue record for this book is available from the British Library

ISBN 9781529931822

To the University of Western Australia, The Western Australian Academy of Performing Arts
(Edith Cowan University) and the Mountview Academy of Theatre Arts...
To Michael Lynch and Caroline Chignell and Katie Minchin...
To everyone at Penguin Random House...
And to Dave Brown and Andrew Rae...
Thanks.

Publishing Director: Albert DePetrillo
Editor: Phoebe Lindsley
Design: Dave Brown
Production: Antony Heller

Printed and bound in Great Britain by Clays Ltd, Elcograf S.p.A.

The authorised representative in the EEA is
Penguin Random House Ireland, Morrison Chambers,
32 Nassau Street, Dublin D02 YH68.

Penguin Random House is committed to a sustainable future
for our business, our readers and our planet. This book is
made from Forest Stewardship Council® certified paper.